EXPERIENCING GOD AS COUPLES

Henry and Marilynn Blackaby

LifeWay.

LifeWay Press
Nashville, Tennessee

ISBN 0-7673-9087-3

Dewey Decimal Classification: 306.81
Subject Heading: MARRIAGE\SPIRITUAL LIFE

This book is the text for course CG-0517
in the subject area Home/Family in the Christian Growth Study Plan.

Unless otherwise noted, Scripture quotations marked (NKJV) are from the
New King James Version. Copyright © 1979, 1980, 1982, Thomas Nelson, Inc., Publishers.

Scripture quotations marked (NIV) are from the Holy Bible, *New International Version,*
copyright © 1973, 1978, 1984 by International Bible Society.

Scripture quotations marked (NASB) are from the NEW AMERICAN STANDARD
BIBLE, © Copyright The Lockman Foundation 1960, 1962, 1963, 1968,
1971, 1972, 1973, 1975, 1977, 1995. Used by permission.

Scripture quotations marked (NEB) are from *The New English Bible.*
Copyright © The Delegates of the Oxford University Press and the Syndics of the
Cambridge University Press, 1961, 1970. Reprinted by permission.

Order additional copies of this book by writing to Customer Service Center, MSN 113;
127 Ninth Avenue, North; Nashville, TN 37234-0113; by calling toll free (800) 458-2772;
by faxing (615) 251-5933; by ordering online at *www.lifeway.com*; by emailing
customerservice@lifeway.com; or by visiting a LifeWay Christian Store.

For information about adult discipleship and family resources, training, and events,
visit our Web site at *www.lifeway.com/discipleplus.*

Printed in the United States of America

LifeWay Press
127 Ninth Avenue, North
Nashville, Tennessee 37234-0151

*As God works through us, we will help people and churches know Jesus Christ and
seek His kingdom by providing biblical solutions that spiritually transform individuals and cultures.*

Contents

Meet the Blackabys 4
Introduction 5

Chapter 1
God at Work in Your Marriage . . . 7
    Couple View 1 8
    Couple Talk 1 11
    Couple Shaper 1 12
    Couple Time 1 17

Chapter 2
God's Love Relationship with
You and Your Spouse 18
    Couple View 2 19
    Couple Talk 2 22
    Couple Shaper 2 23
    Couple Time 2 28

Chapter 3
God Invites You as a Couple to
Become Involved in His Work . . .29
    Couple View 3 30
    Couple Talk 3 33
    Couple Shaper 3 34
    Couple Time 3 39

Chapter 4
God's Ways of Speaking to
You as a Couple 40
    Couple View 4 41
    Couple Talk 4 44
    Couple Shaper 4 45
    Couple Time 4 50

Chapter 5
Experiencing a Crisis of Belief
in Your Marriage 51
    Couple View 5 52
    Couple Talk 5 55
    Couple Shaper 5 56
    Couple Time 5 61

Chapter 6
Adjusting to God's Will for
Your Marriage 62
    Couple View 6 63
    Couple Talk 6 66
    Couple Shaper 6 67
    Couple Time 6 71

Chapter 7
Allowing God to Work Through
Your Marriage 72
    Couple View 7 73
    Couple Talk 7 77
    Couple Shaper 7 78
    Couple Time 7 82

Chapter 8
Committing to a Covenant
Marriage 83
    Couple View 8 84
    Couple Talk 8 86
    Couple Shaper 8 87
    Couple Time 8 93

Christian Growth Study Plan . .95

Meet the Blackabys

*H*enry Blackaby is Director of the Office of Prayer and Spiritual Awakening at the North American Mission Board in Atlanta, Georgia. He provides consultative leadership on prayer for revival and spiritual awakening in the life of the Southern Baptist Convention. Henry also serves as consultant to the International Mission Board and LifeWay Christian Resources on prayer and spiritual awakening for global revival. Henry's wife Marilynn ministers by his side as she has throughout their 35 plus years of marriage.

Henry is a native Canadian; Marilynn was born in Tulsa, Oklahoma. Prior to accepting his current position, Henry was Director of Missions for Capilano Baptist Association, Canada, serving under missionary appointment by the North American Mission Board's Metropolitan Missions Department.

The Blackabys have five grown children, four sons and one daughter, all serving in the ministry. Henry and Marilynn currently live in Atlanta, Georgia.

Introduction

Welcome to *Experiencing God as Couples*! By choosing to participate in this study, you are demonstrating your commitment to apply biblical principles to your marriage relationship.

Experiencing God as Couples began as Experiencing God Weekends for Couples. Henry and Marilynn Blackaby lead several of these weekends each year. To broaden the reach of their message, this video-based course was produced. The study takes the seven realities of experiencing God and applies each one to the marriage relationship.

The message of *Experiencing God as Couples* is contained in the video presentations. This book supports that material. As you work through this book, there are several terms you will encounter. Your study will make more sense if you become familiar with those terms ahead of time.

Couple View–A viewer's guide to be used while watching the video presentations.

Couple Talk–Discussion questions based on the material in each video presentation. These questions can be used in a small-group meeting at your church, in a home, or in another setting in your community. The questions can also be used with another couple.

Couple Shaper–A personal study section expanding the content of the video presentation. This material is to be used after Couple View and Couple Talk. You will benefit more by working through this section individually before sharing with your spouse.

Couple Time–Practical activities to be discussed and completed with your spouse after each of you have completed Couple Shaper.

As you begin your study of *Experiencing God as Couples*, consider the following suggestions. Each one will make your study more meaningful for you and your spouse. Check the box by those you will commit to complete.

❑ Ask the Holy Spirit for guidance; commit to be obedient to what He teaches you.
❑ Spend time in earnest prayer both alone and with your spouse.
❑ Spend time meditating on and discussing with your spouse and other couples what God is revealing to you.
❑ Use the designated pages in this book to keep a journal of what the Lord is teaching you. In years to come, the journal will remind you of things your memory won't.
❑ Expect God to honor your faithful obedience.

To gain the most from *Experiencing God as Couples*, it is important that you and your spouse participate in all parts of the study. View each video presentation, participate in the discussion with a small group or another couple, spend time in personal study, and commit to spending time together as a couple. These parts are designed to challenge you and help you draw application from what God has to say.

If you are forming a group of couples to participate in the study, watch the leader segment of the video. Use the promotional video segments in your enlistment. The longer version can be shown in large meetings and set up to be viewed in hallways—wherever couples congregate. The shorter segment can be used on local television networks to reach couples in your community. Add your own message on the end indicating how they can get more information.

May God bless you in your study as you experience Him as a couple.

Session 1

God at Work in Your Marriage

REALITY 1
God is always at work around you.

Jesus answered them, "My Father has been working
until now, and I have been working."
–John 5:17

Couple View 1

✢ **Foundational Truth:** *Long before you become aware of what God is doing, He is at work in your life.*

"Jesus answered them, 'My Father has been working until now, and I have been working.'... Then Jesus answered and said to them, 'Most assuredly, I say to you, the Son can do nothing of Himself, but what He sees the Father do; for whatever He does, the Son also does in like manner. For the Father loves the Son, and shows Him all things that He Himself does; and He will show Him greater works than these, that you may marvel' " (John 5:17,19-20).

Your heritage provides a clue to the _____

_____ for your life.

It's important to share your _____ with your spouse.

You are responsible for helping your spouse fulfill his or her

_____ to God.

God gives you children with definite _____ for
their lives.

God has _____ been at work in your life
and your marriage.

Children must be _____ that God has a
special purpose for their lives.

Your experiences are _____ _____
to where God is leading you.

"Yet you say, 'For what reason?' Because the Lord has been witness
between you and the wife of your youth, with whom you have
dealt treacherously; yet she is your companion and your wife by
covenant. But did He not make them one, having a remnant of the
Spirit? And why one? He seeks godly offspring. Therefore take heed
to your spirit, and let none deal treacherously with the wife of his
youth" (Mal. 2:14-15).

God makes a married couple one in flesh and one in

_____

" 'I say to you, he who receives whomever I send receives Me; and he who receives Me receives Him who sent Me' " (John 13:20).

How you _____ your spouse is the same as how you

_____ God.

Recognize and record God's activity in your life as

_____ _____.

Couple Talk 1

✤ **Use the following as a guide to talk with another couple or a small group of couples. Pray together as you begin your discussion.**

1. Reality 1 says: *God is always at work around you.* What one thing from your life has demonstrated this reality that you would be willing to share with the group?

2. In a round-robin format, make a list of words or phrases that define a self-centered life. When everyone has contributed, do the same to define a God-centered life. You will compare these later with the lists in Couple Shaper 1.

Self-Centered Life	*God-Centered Life*
me	always seeking
pride	humble
manipulation	giving
taking	loving

3. What has God taught you through your family of origin that you have brought to your marriage relationship? tithing, going to church, family

4. How has God demonstrated His presence and/or activity in your life or your marriage? It may help to reflect on an occasion when something occurred that, apart from God's presence, would have had no other explanation. Writing songs, healing, God's presence in my prayers.

5. How you receive your spouse is the same as how you receive God. What practical application does this have for your marriage relationship? Believing in each other

6. When God gets ready for you to take a new step or direction in His activity, it will always be in sequence with what He has already been doing in your life. Share some spiritual markers in your life. How can the use of spiritual markers help you make an important decision in your life? … in your marriage?

Jeff's music — how the songs came about and then were recorded.

Couple Shaper 1

Reality 1: *God is always at work around you.*

Thoughts from Experiencing God
- To know God and do the will of God, you must deny self and return to a God-centered life.
- Understanding what God is about to do where you are is more important than telling God what you want to do for Him.
- God's revelation of His activity is an invitation for you to join Him.
- God has not changed. He still speaks to His people.
- God develops character to match the assignment.
- To understand your bad or difficult circumstances, God's perspective is vital.
- When God gets ready for you to take a new step or direction in His activity, it will always be in sequence with what He has already been doing in your life.

God-Centered Living
When we deny self and center our lives on God, He can accomplish through us His purposes. Compare the following lists with those developed in Couple Talk 1.

Self-Centered Life	*God-Centered Life*
• life focused on self	• life focused on God and His activity
• proud of self and self's accomplishments	• humble before God
• self confident	• confident in God
• dependence on self and one's own abilities	• dependence on God and His ability and provision
• affirming self	• denying self
• seeking to be acceptable to the world's ways	• seeking the kingdom of God and His righteousness
• looking at circumstances from a human view	• seeking God's perspective in every circumstance
• selfish and ordinary living	• holy and godly living

Which life are you living?
❏ Self-centered life   ❏ God-centered life   ❏ Unsure

In your own words, describe a marriage partner who lives a God-centered life.

_____

_____

_____

Spiritual Markers

"One thing I have found helpful is to identify 'spiritual markers' in my life. Each time I have encountered God's call or directions for my life, I have mentally built a spiritual marker at that point. A spiritual marker identifies a time of transition, decision, or direction when I clearly know that God has guided me. Over time I can look back at these spiritual markers and see how God has faithfully directed my life according to His divine purpose."[1]

Identify your spiritual markers. These might include moments from your past, your salvation experience, times you made significant decisions that determined your future, and so on. The basic question is: What times can you identify in your life when you knew without a doubt that God guided you? Begin with prayer, asking God to bring those times to your mind. Then write a brief description of each experience.

_____

_____

_____

_____

_____

_____

_____

Sharing Your Spiritual Heritage

God has always been at work in your life and your marriage. Your experiences are foundational points to where God is leading you. So it's important to share your spiritual heritage with your spouse and your children. Write a letter to your spouse telling how God has worked in your life. Make it personal. You will share your letter with your spouse during Couple Time.

_____

_____

_____

_____

_____

_____

_____

_____

Experiencing God as Couples Journal

What statement or Scripture in the video session has God used to speak to you about Himself, His purposes, or His ways?

_____

_____

_____

_____

_____

_____

_____

_____

Personalize the statement or Scripture by rewording it to reflect application to your marriage.

_____

_____

_____

_____

_____

_____

_____

_____

What adjustment is God leading you to make in response to what He has said to you?

_____

_____

_____

_____

_____

_____

_____

_____

_____

_____

How have you demonstrated your obedience to God this week?

_____

_____

_____

_____

_____

_____

What particular person or concern has God given you a burden to pray with your spouse about?

_____

_____

_____

_____

_____

_____

_____

_____

---

[1]Henry T. Blackaby and Claude V. King, _Experiencing God: Knowing and Doing the Will of God_ (Nashville: LifeWay Press, 1990), 103.

Couple Time 1

1. What did you bring from your past to your marriage? Answer this question with your spouse and make a list below.

What I brought to our marriage: **What you brought to our marriage:**

_____   _____

_____   _____

_____   _____

_____   _____

_____   _____

2. Each of you made a list of spiritual markers during Couple Shaper 1. Share the letters you wrote telling how God has worked in your life. Then, identify your spiritual markers as a couple. What times can you identify in your life as a couple when you knew without a doubt that God guided you? Begin with prayer, asking God to bring those times to your mind. Then together write a brief description on a separate sheet of paper of each experience.

3. Ask your spouse: What are your commitments to God? How am I helping you fulfill those commitments? Be sensitive to what your spouse shares. Pray that God will show you specific ways to help him/her fulfill those commitments in the days ahead.

4. Share with each other what you recorded in your *Experiencing God as Couples Journal*. Close your time together in prayer for each other and your marriage.

God's Love Relationship with You and Your Spouse

REALITY 2
God pursues a love relationship with you that is real and personal.

Now before the Feast of the Passover, Jesus knew that His hour had come that He should depart from this world to the Father, having loved His own who were in the world, He loved them to the end."

—John 13:1

Couple View 2

" 'For God so loved the world that He gave His only begotten Son, that whosoever believes in Him should not perish but have everlasting life' " (John 3:16).

"By this we know love, because He laid down His life for us. And we also ought to lay down our lives for the brethren" (1 John 3:16).

To follow Christ's example, we must _____ _____

our lives for our families.

"Having loved His own who were in the world, He loved them to the end" (John 13:1).

Your love as a spouse/parent must _____ and

_____ with every passing day.

As you live your life as a couple, the Lord will _____

His love for you.

Marital love should be _____, as God's love is for us.

New Testament examples of God's _____ show how a

couple should _____ love for one another.

Your love must _____ your spouse all the time, just

as God's _____ always pursues you.

" 'A new commandment I give to you, that you love one another; as I have loved you, that you also love one another' " (John 13:34).

" 'Call to Me, and I will answer you, and show you great and mighty things, which you do not know' " (Jeremiah 33:3).

God will show you _____ and _____

things in and through your marriage.

God will always be _____ to you.

God's love for you never _____, never _____,

always _____.

God will make _____ out of your most

_____ moments if you allow His love to pursue you.

Revisit difficult moments in your married life and _____

at them from God's _____.

Let God remind you of the moments you may have interpreted as negative. Redefine.

Reinterpret your marriage relationship in terms of God's love. God's love transforms any situation.

Couple Talk 2

✣ **Use the following as a guide to talk with another couple or a small group of couples. Pray together as you begin your discussion.**

1. Reality 2 says: *God pursues a love relationship with you that is real and personal.* What one thing from your life has demonstrated this reality that you would be willing to share with the group?

2. The following Scriptures speak of a love relationship. Read them in your Bible and then answer the questions.

   • John 3:16
   • John 14:21
   • Romans 8:35,37,39
   • 1 John 3:16
   • 1 John 4:9-10,19

In what ways has God demonstrated His love for us? How can we show our love for Him? What does God promise to do in response to our loving Him?

3. The following Scriptures speak of God's initiative in the love relationship. Read each passage in your Bible and identify phrases that speak of God's initiative.

   • John 15:16
   • Philippians 2:13
   • Revelation 3:20

4. One way God pursues a love relationship with you is through your spouse. Share an example from your marriage that illustrates this statement.

5. How has God pursued a love relationship with you as a couple? Share an experience or time in your marriage when God demonstrated His love in a real, personal, and/or practical way.

Couple Shaper 2

Reality 2: *God pursues a love relationship with you that is real and personal.*

Thoughts from **Experiencing God**
- A love relationship with God is more important than any other single factor in your life.
- Everything God says and does is an expression of love.
- To be loved by God is the highest relationship, the highest achievement, and the highest position of your life.
- When your relationship is as it ought to be, you will always be in fellowship with the Father.
- God takes the initiative. He chooses us, loves us, and reveals His eternal purposes for our lives.
- God's plan for the advancement of His kingdom depends on His working in real and practical ways through His personal relationship with His people.

Laying Down Our Lives
How do we know love? "By this we know love, because He laid down His life for us. And we also ought to lay down our lives for the brethren" (1 John 3:16). To follow Christ's example, we must lay down our lives for our families. Identify practical ways you can lay down your life for …

… your spouse _____

_____

_____

… your children _____

_____

_____

23

Marital Love Is Forever

Christ's love for us is the model for our love for our spouse. One characteristic is that it is forever. Marriage is a no-looking-back, no-turning-back commitment. Jesus emphasized that marriage is to be a permanent union. " 'What God has joined together, man must not separate' " (Mark 10:9, NEB).

Describe a marriage where the husband and wife are committed to standing by each other forever no matter what life may bring.

_____

_____

_____

_____

_____

God's Love in Your Marriage

God will show you great and mighty things in and through your marriage. God will make positives out of your most difficult moments if you allow His love to pursue you. Revisit difficult moments in your married life and look at them from God's perspective. Describe in the first column three times in your married life that you considered negative experiences. Redefine them in the second column by identifying ways God's love was expressed for you as a couple.

From Our Perspective	From God's Perspective
1. _____	_____
_____	_____
_____	_____
_____	_____

2.. _____   _____

  _____   _____

  _____   _____

  _____   _____

3.. _____   _____

  _____   _____

  _____   _____

  _____   _____

Experiencing God as Couples Journal
What statement or Scripture in the video session has God used to speak to you about Himself, His purposes, or His ways?

_____

_____

_____

_____

_____

_____

_____

_____

Personalize the statement or Scripture by rewording it to reflect application to your marriage.

_____

_____

_____

_____

_____

_____

_____

What adjustment is God leading you to make in response to what He has said to you?

_____

_____

_____

_____

_____

_____

_____

_____

How have you demonstrated your obedience to God this week?

_____

_____

_____

_____

_____

_____

_____

What particular person or concern has God given you a burden to pray with your spouse about?

_____

_____

_____

_____

_____

_____

_____

Couple Time 2

1. Answer the following questions as a couple. Take notes in the space provided.

• In what ways has God demonstrated His love for us?

_____

_____

• How can we show our love as a couple for Him?

_____

_____

2. Each of you identified practical ways you lay down your life for your spouse and your children. Share your ideas with each other. Pray, thanking God for the love relationship you share together and for the example of God's love for you.

3. Ask your spouse: How did you describe a marriage where the husband and wife are committed to a life together forever? Compare each of your descriptions from Couple Shaper 2.

4. Read together Jeremiah 33:3. Revisit the lists you made of difficult moments in your married life that you redefined in terms of God performing "great and mighty things" you may or may not have recognized at the time.

5. Share with each other what you recorded in your *Experiencing God as Couples Journal*. Close your time together in prayer for each other and your marriage.

God Invites You as a Couple to Become Involved in His Work

REALITY 3
*God invites you to become involved with
Him in His work.*

Then He said to them all, "If anyone desires to come after Me,
Let him deny himself, and take up his cross daily,
and follow Me." —Luke 9:23

Couple View 3

God always _____ you to join Him in what He is doing.

" 'And when he brings out his own sheep, he goes before them; and the sheep follow him, for they know his voice' " (John 10:4).

"Then He said to them all, 'If anyone desires to come after Me, let him deny himself, and take up his cross daily, and follow Me' " (Luke 9:23).

A couple must _____ themselves, _____ _____

their cross, and _____ Him.

What are you doing in _____ the Lord in your home

and your marriage?

" 'I say to you, unless a grain of wheat falls into the ground and dies, it remains alone; but if it dies, it produces much grain' " (John 12:24).

By _____ to self, a couple can _____ God in what

He is already doing in their home.

God wants us to _____ the _____ of

His joy in our homes.

" 'You are My friends if you do whatever I command you' "
(John 15:14).

God invites couples to go on _____ with Him to

_____ lives.

"He shall be like a tree planted by the rivers of water, that brings forth
its fruit in its season, whose leaf also shall not wither; and whatever
he does shall prosper" (Psalm 1:3).

God _____ _____ to the end those things He

_____.

Responding to God's invitation to join Him will _____

your entire family.

If you are where God is, everything is _____.

Couple Talk 3

✢ **Use the following as a guide to talk with another couple or a small group of couples. Pray together as you begin your discussion.**

1. Reality 3 says: *God invites you to become involved with Him in His work.* What one thing from your life demonstrates this reality that you would be willing to share with the group?

2. God did not create you for time—He created you for an eternal love relationship with Him. The psalmist proclaims this beautifully in Psalm 139, and the prophet Jeremiah said it well in Jeremiah 1:5. Read these passages of Scripture aloud. Do you believe God, who is love, is that involved in your life? In what ways is that evident in your life?

3. Read Luke 9:23. What does it mean to "deny himself"? What does it mean to "take up his cross"? Henry Blackaby said, "God didn't send me off; He said 'follow me.' " What does it mean to "follow me"? How does all of this apply in a marriage relationship?

4. What is God doing in your home? How can you join God in what He is doing? What impact will that have on your marriage and family?

5. God sees to the end what He initiates. Share testimonies in your group that expresses the truth in that statement. Close this sharing time by reading Psalm 1:3.

Couple Shaper 3

Reality 3: *God invites you to become involved with Him in His work.*

Thoughts from Experiencing God

- Knowing God only comes through your experiences with Him as He reveals Himself.
- God is love. His will is always best.
- God is all-knowing. His directions are always right.
- God is all-powerful. He can enable you to do His will.
- When you see the Father at work around you, that is your invitation to adjust your life to Him and join Him in that work.
- A tender and sensitive heart will be ready to respond to God at the slightest prompting.
- What God initiates, He completes.

Knowing God

You come to know God more intimately as He reveals Himself to you through your experiences with Him. Read the following lists of names, titles, and descriptions of God. Circle those that describe God in ways you and your spouse have experienced Him in your marriage. Write a sentence in the space provided briefly identifying the experience.

- Comforter in sorrow (Jer. 8:18) _____

_____

- Wonderful Counselor (Isa. 9:6) _____

_____

- A sure foundation (Isa. 28:16) _____

_____

• Our guide (Ps. 48:14) _____

_____

• Faithful and true (Rev. 19:11) _____

_____

• My hiding place (Ps. 32:7) _____

_____

• My hope (Ps. 71:5) _____

_____

• Good teacher (Mark 10:17) _____

_____

• Our peace (Eph. 2:14) _____

_____

• Refuge and strength (Ps. 46:1) _____

_____

Deny, Take Up, Follow

Just as we are to do it individually, a couple must deny themselves, take up their cross, and follow Jesus. List ways you are doing that as a couple in your marriage.

Deny: _____

_____

Take Up: _____

_____

Follow: _____

_____

God's Invitation

By dying to self, a couple can join God in what He is already doing in their home. Focus on your present home life and answer the following questions.

1. What is God doing in your marriage and family right now?

_____

_____

_____

2. What are you and your spouse doing in following the Lord in your home and in your marriage?

_____

_____

_____

_____

3. Do you feel you are on mission with God where you are now? ❑ Yes ❑ No ❑ Unsure   What are your dreams and aspirations? What will you do to be on mission with God?

_____

_____

_____

Experiencing God as Couples Journal
What statement or Scripture in the video session has God used to speak to you about Himself, His purposes, or His ways?

_____

_____

_____

_____

_____

_____

_____

Personalize the statement or Scripture by rewording it to reflect application to your marriage.

_____

_____

_____

_____

_____

_____

_____

_____

What adjustment is God leading you to make in response to what He has said to you?

_____

_____

_____

_____

_____

_____

How have you demonstrated your obedience to God this week?

_____

_____

_____

_____

What particular person or concern has God given you a burden to pray with your spouse about?

_____

_____

_____

_____

Couple Time 3

1. Review together the names, titles, and descriptions of God that each of you selected to describe experiences you have had with God in your marriage. Write your spouse's selections and thoughts below.

_____

_____

_____

2. Each of you made lists of ways you are denying yourself, taking up your cross, and following Jesus. Compare those with each other and discuss other ways to accomplish them in your daily life. List your new ideas below.

_____

_____

3. Using your answer to the three questions under "God's Invitation" in Couple Shaper 3, identify how you as a couple can be on mission with God based on His activity in your marriage and family. Pray for a tender and sensitive heart as you identify what God is doing and how you can join Him. Write your thoughts below.

_____

_____

4. Share with each other what you recorded in your *Experiencing God as Couples Journal*. Close your time together in prayer for each other and your marriage.

Session 4

God's Ways of Speaking to You as a Couple

REALITY 4

God speaks by the Holy Spirit through the Bible, prayer, circumstances, and the church to reveal Himself, His purposes, and His ways.

He who is of God hears God's words; therefore you do not hear, because you are not of God. —John 8:47

Couple View 4

Reality 1: *God is always at* _____ *around you.*

"Surely the Lord God does nothing, unless He reveals His secret to His servants the prophets" (Amos 3:7).

Reality 2: *God pursues a* _____ *relationship with you that is* _____ *and* _____.

When God speaks to you as a couple, it is always _____ _____ for you.

Reality 3: *God invites you to become* _____ *with Him in His work.*

The Bible tells you how to _____ to how God _____ to you.

It is far more difficult _____ _____ _____ God than to _____ Him.

A Scriptural truth is that God _____ with His people.

God speaks by the _____ _____.

The Holy Spirit will teach you _____ things and guide you

in _____ truth.

"You shall love the Lord your God with all your heart, with all your soul, and with all your strength. And these words, which I command you today shall be in your heart" (Deut. 6:5-6).

How you as a couple are _____ is a clear indication

of whether biblical truth has gone from your _____

to your _____.

"You shall teach them diligently to your children, and shall talk of them when you sit in your house, when you walk by the way, when you lie down, and when you rise up. You shall bind them as a sign on your hand, and they shall be as frontlets between your eyes. You shall write them on the doorposts of your house and on your gates" (Deut. 6:7-9).

"When Jesus heard that, He said, 'This sickness is not unto death, but for the glory of God, that the Son of God may be glorified through it' " (John 11:4).

Sometimes God allows families to go through the _____

of a crisis to _____ them more about Himself.

"Let your conduct be without covetousness; be content with such things as you have. For He Himself has said, 'I will never leave you nor forsake you' " (Heb. 13:5).

Be _____ to the needs of your family and

_____ immediately for them.

Even when you cannot reach your family, you always have

_____ to the Lord.

" 'When he brings out his own sheep, he goes before them; and the sheep follow him, for they know his voice' " (John 10:4).

When God _____ to you through the Bible and

prayer, _____ it with your children.

When you as a couple need a _____ _____

from the Lord, learn to _____ His voice.

Couple Talk 4

❖ **Use the following as a guide to talk with another couple or a small group of couples. Pray together as you begin your discussion.**

1. Reality 4 says: *God speaks by the Holy Spirit through the Bible, prayer, circumstances, and the church to reveal Himself, His purposes, and His ways.* What one thing from your life demonstrates this reality that you would be willing to share with the group?

2. We read in Scripture and have heard people testify that there are certain things only God can do. If we sense these things happening, we can rest assured it is God's activity and we need to be obedient to what He is saying to us. What are these things? Review the following categories and share personal examples for each one.

- God draws people to Himself.
- God causes people to seek after Him.
- God reveals spiritual truth.
- God convicts the world of guilt regarding sin.
- God convicts the world of righteousness.
- God convicts the world of judgment.

3. God's Holy Spirit uses the Word of God to instruct us in the ways of God. On our own we cannot understand the truths of God. Read aloud 1 Corinthians 2:14-15. Use the following statement to discuss how we understand spiritual truth. *Understanding spiritual truth does not lead you to an encounter with God, it is the encounter with God.*

4. God's Holy Spirit uses the Word of God to guide you in the area of your praying. We are weak and do not know how we ought to pray. Read aloud Romans 8:26-27. Share personal experiences of when the Spirit led you to prayer for an individual or concern.

5. God will speak to you through your spouse. Identify a time when God spoke to you through your spouse? Share it with the group. Were you receptive? Were you obedient to God?

Couple Shaper 4

Reality 4: *God speaks by the Holy Spirit through the Bible, prayer, circumstances, and the church to reveal Himself, His purposes, and His ways.*

Thoughts from Experiencing God
- God speaks to His people.
- If you do not know when God is speaking, you are in trouble at the heart of your Christian life.
- *That* God speaks to people is far more important than *how* He speaks.
- An encounter with the Holy Spirit is an encounter with God.
- God's revelations are designed to bring you into a love relationship with Him.
- The Spirit of God uses the Word of God to reveal God and His purposes.
- Prayer is a relationship with God, not just a religious activity.

God Speaks
God speaks to His people. How? Mark the following statements as T (True) or F (False).

_____ 1. God can uniquely speak to individuals any way He chooses.

_____ 2. In the present, God primarily speaks through dreams and visions.

_____ 3. When rightly related to God, His people will hear and recognize His voice.

_____ 4. God frequently speaks by the Holy Spirit through the Bible and prayer.

Only item 2 is false. The others are true. In the present, God primarily speaks by the Holy Spirit through the Bible, prayer, circumstances, and the church.

45

God Speaks Through the Bible
How do you personally respond to a word from God from Scripture?

_____

_____

How do you as a couple respond to a word from God from Scripture?

_____

_____

Both of these questions assume you and your spouse are spending time in God's Word. If you are not doing this, what adjustments would have to be made in your lives to spend time regularly in God's Word?

_____

_____

When God leads you and your spouse to a fresh understanding of Himself or His ways through Scripture:
1. Write down the verse(s).
2. Meditate on the verse(s).
3. Study it to immerse yourself in its meaning.
4. Identify the adjustments you need to make in your personal life, your marriage and family, your church, and your work.
5. Write a prayer response to God.
6. Make the necessary adjustment.
7. Watch to see how God may use the truth in your daily life.

God Speaks Through Prayer
Prayer is a two-way fellowship and communication with God. You speak to God and God speaks to you. Prayer is designed more to adjust you to God than to adjust God to you. God doesn't need your prayers, but He wants you to pray. You need to pray because of what God wants to do in and through your life.

Read Romans 8:26-27 below and underline the words or phrases that answer the following questions.

"Likewise the Spirit also helps in our weaknesses. For we do not know what we should pray for as we ought, but the Spirit Himself makes intercession for us with groanings which cannot be uttered. Now He who searches the hearts knows what the mind of the Spirit is, because He makes intercession for the saints according to the will of God" (Rom.8:26-27).

1. Why do we need the Holy Spirit when we pray?
2. What advantages does the Holy Spirit have that we do not have?
3. What does the Spirit do for us?

Has God spoken to you recently through prayer about a family matter? Briefly describe what you sensed He was saying and how you responded.

_____

_____

_____

Experiencing God as Couples Journal
What statement or Scripture in the video session has God used to speak to you about Himself, His purposes, or His ways?

_____

_____

_____

_____

_____

_____

Personalize the statement or Scripture by rewording it to reflect application to your marriage.

_____

_____

_____

_____

_____

_____

_____

What adjustment is God leading you to make in response to what He has said to you?

_____

_____

_____

_____

_____

_____

_____

How have you demonstrated your obedience to God this week?

_____

_____

_____

_____

_____

_____

What particular person or concern has God given you a burden to pray with your spouse about?

_____

_____

_____

_____

_____

_____

Couple Time 4

1. How does God speak to you as a couple? Discuss specific ways God has spoken to you concerning your marriage and family. How has God's Holy Spirit guided you in key family decisions? How has God brought comfort and peace during times of loss and crisis?

2. Evaluate the amount of time and the regularity of time spent in God's Word. Share what you listed in Couple Shaper 4 concerning adjustments you would have to make in your lives to spend more time regularly in God's Word.

3. Sometimes God allows families to go through a crisis to allow them to know Him on a more intimate level. Can you identify a time in your marriage when that seemed to be the case? Talk about this with your spouse and briefly describe the situation and what God taught you.

_____

_____

_____

_____

4. When God speaks to you as a couple through the Bible and prayer, share it with your children. Have you done that lately? Over the next several weeks, establish the habit of doing that by consciously telling your children what God is saying to you. Help them understand the importance of obeying God when He speaks.

5. Share with each other what you recorded in your *Experiencing God as Couples Journal*. Close your time together in prayer for each other and your marriage.

Experiencing a Crisis of Belief in Your Marriage

REALITY 5
God's invitation for you to work with Him always leads you to a crisis of belief that requires faith and action.

Without faith it is impossible to please Him, for he who comes to God must believe that He is, and that He is a rewarder of those who diligently seek Him.

–Hebrews 11:6

Couple View 5

"Then they said to Him, 'What shall we do, that we may work the works of God?' Jesus answered and said to them, 'This is the work of God, that you believe in Him whom He sent' " (John 6:28-29).

You can postpone a response to a _____,

but postponing a response to _____ is to say, "_____!"

_____ obedience to God is _____.

When God speaks to you, whatever you do next _____

what you _____ about Him.

When God's _____ is not what you wanted, your

decision to discuss it is really _____.

Whenever God _____ you to do something, it will

always be _____ what you can do on your own.

"The Lord said to Gideon, 'The people who are with you are too many for Me to give the Midianites into their hands, lest Israel claim glory for itself against Me, saying "My own hand has saved me." Now therefore, proclaim in the hearing of the people, saying, "Whoever is fearful and afraid, let him turn and depart at once from Mount Gilead." And twenty-two thousand of the people returned, and ten thousand remained.

But the Lord said to Gideon, 'The people are still too many; bring them down to the water, and I will test them for you there. Then it will be that of whom I say to you, "This one shall go with you," the same shall go with you; and of whomever I say to you, "This one shall not go with you," the same shall not go.' So he brought the people down to the water. And the Lord said to Gideon, 'everyone who laps from the water with his tongue, as a dog laps, you shall set apart by himself; likewise everyone who gets down on his knees to drink.' And the number of those who lapped, putting their hand to their mouth, was three hundred men; but all the rest of the people got down on their knees to drink water. Then the Lord said to Gideon, 'By the three hundred men who lapped I will save you, and deliver the Midianites into your hand. Let all the other people go, every man to his place' " (Judges 7:2-7).

"Putting out the _____" to determine God's will is an

act of unbelief.

When God _____ Himself to you as a couple, He requires

an immediate response of _____.

If God tells you to do something about your crisis, He will

be working on the _____ _____ of the situation, too.

When you come to the Scripture and pray, you will face a

_____ of _____ when God encounters you.

Do you _____ what God says is true?

Will you make an _____ in your life to God?

There is no _____ person or situation with God.

Your crisis may require you to _____ _____ of God's way so He can work in it.

God will keep leading you to a crisis of belief so you can go on to the _____ _____ of faith.

Neither you nor your marriage can _____ in faith unless God takes you _____ your last expression of faith.

A crisis of belief doesn't come because you _____ _____ the will of God; it comes because you _____ _____ the will of God.

Couple Talk 5

✤ **Use the following as a guide to talk with another couple or a small group of couples. Pray together as you begin your discussion.**

1. Reality 5 says: *God's invitation for you to work with Him always leads you to a crisis of belief that requires faith and action.* What one thing from your life has demonstrated this reality that you would be willing to share with the group?

2. Whenever God asks you to do something, it will always be beyond what you can do on your own. Share with the group about a time when that has been evident in your marriage.

3. Based on what you experienced during the video session, define a crisis of belief. Take notes below as group members express their thoughts.

_____

_____

_____

_____

4. Given your understanding of what is meant by a crisis of belief, tell about a crisis of belief you and your spouse have experienced. How did your crisis of belief help you move to the next step of faith?

5. What you do in response to God's invitation to join Him reveals what you believe about God. What did you and your spouse do as a response to your crisis of belief? What were the results?

6. Close with a prayer acknowledging that neither you nor your marriage can grow in faith unless God takes you beyond your last expression of faith.

Couple Shaper 5

Reality 5: *God's invitation for you to work with Him always leads you to a crisis of belief that requires faith and action.*

Thoughts from Experiencing God
- An encounter with God requires faith.
- Encounters with God are God-sized.
- What you do in response to God's invitation reveals what you believe about God.
- What you believe about God determines what you do and how you live.
- True faith requires action.
- Faith is believing that the God who calls us to an assignment is the One who provides for its accomplishment.
- Don't grow weary in being faithful; a reward awaits faithful servants.

Crisis of Belief
God's Word contains many examples of people facing a crisis of belief. Look in your Bible in Matthew at the following examples. Identify the person and his or her crisis of belief. Then describe what each person did in response to God.

	Person	Crisis of Belief	Response
Matthew 8:5-13			
Matthew 8:23-27			
Matthew 9:20-22			
Matthew 9:27-31			

When the two blind men demonstrated that they believed Jesus was merciful and that He was the Messiah, Jesus healed them according to their faith. The woman believed that just a touch of Jesus' garment would allow His healing power to flow to her. She was willing to risk public ridicule in order to experience His healing power. When the storms of life overtake us like the storm overtook the disciples, we often respond as if God does not exist or does not care. Jesus rebuked them, not for their fear, but for their failure to recognize His presence, protection, and power. "Just say the word, and my servant will be healed," the centurion claimed. Jesus commended the centurion's faith in His authority and power. What each of these people did indicated what kind of faith they had in Jesus.

Faith
When God speaks, your response require faith. Read the following Scripture passages and underline the word faith each time it appears.

"Now faith is the substance of things hoped for, the evidence of things not seen" (Heb. 11:1).

"Without faith it is impossible to please Him, for he who comes to God must believe that He is, and that He is a rewarder of those who diligently seek Him" (Heb. 11:6).

"For we walk by faith, not by sight" (2 Cor. 5:7).

" 'Most assuredly, I say to you, he who believes in Me, the words that I do he will do also; and greater works than these he will do, because I go to My Father' " (John 14:12).

"So Jesus said to them, 'Because of your unbelief; for assuredly, I say to you, if you have faith as a mustard seed, you will say to this mountain, "Move from here to there," and it will move; and nothing will be impossible for you' " (Matt. 17:20-21).

" 'The head of Ephraim is Samaria, and the head of Samaria is Remaliah's son. If you will not believe, surely you shall not be established' " (Isa. 7:9).

Based on what you just read, what are the characteristics of faith? List them below.

_____   _____

_____   _____

_____   _____

Faith is confidence that what God has promised or said will come to pass, and that the God who calls us to an assignment will provide for its accomplishment.

Describe a time in your life that required faith. How did you respond?

_____

_____

_____

_____

Action and Results
"As the body without the spirit is dead, so faith without works is dead also" (James 2:26). True faith requires action.

Hebrews 11 is often called "The Roll Call of Faith." Read Hebrews 11:1-38 in your Bible.

Notice that a faithful life does not always bring the same results in human terms. Outward appearances of success do not always indicate faith, and outward appearances of failure do not always indicate a lack of faith. A faithful servant does what His Master tells him, whatever the outcome may be. Jesus endured the cross, but now He is seated near God. What a reward for faithfulness!

Experiencing God as Couples Journal
What statement or Scripture in the video session has God used to speak to you about Himself, His purposes, or His ways?

_____

_____

_____

_____

_____

_____

_____

_____

Personalize the statement or Scripture by rewording it to reflect application to your marriage.

_____

_____

_____

_____

_____

_____

_____

What adjustment is God leading you to make in response to what He has said to you?

_____

_____

_____

_____

_____

_____

How have you demonstrated your obedience to God this week?

_____

_____

_____

_____

_____

What particular person or concern has God given you a burden to pray with your spouse about?

_____

_____

_____

_____

_____

Couple Time 5

1. Just as you completed the chart in Couple Shaper 5 that used biblical illustrations of people facing a crisis of belief, reflect on your past and complete the following chart with your spouse.

	Crisis of Belief	Date or Period	Our Response
1.	_____	_____	_____
	_____	_____	_____
2.	_____	_____	_____
	_____	_____	_____
3.	_____	_____	_____
	_____	_____	_____

2. Have you and your spouse ever expressed your unbelief by "putting out the fleece" to determine God's will? Have you reached the point in your life and marriage when all you need is for God to speak to you and that is sufficient?

3. You and your spouse may be facing a crisis of belief with your children, your future, or your health. Are you ready for God to make His will known to you? Do you believe? Will you live your life in faith that God will lead you to a greater level of trust in Him and that He will never lead you where He will not provide for you?

4. Share with each other what you recorded in your *Experiencing God as Couples Journal*. Close your time together in prayer for each other and your marriage.

Adjusting to God's Will for Your Marriage

REALITY 6
*You must make major adjustments in your life
to join God in what He is doing.*

So likewise, whoever of you does not forsake all
that he has cannot be My disciple.
–Luke 14:33

Couple View 6

Our problem is not _____ what God is asking of us, but

_____ what God is asking and being willing to make

the necessary _____ to be where God is at work.

Don't let _____ determine the will of God; let

the will of God determine your _____.

"He who loves father or mother more than Me is not worthy of Me. And he who loves son or daughter more than Me is not worthy of Me. And he who does not take his cross and follow after Me is not worthy of Me. He who finds his life will lose it, and he who loses his life for My sake will find it" (Matt. 10:37-39).

"Most assuredly, I say to you, unless a grain of wheat falls into the ground and dies, it remains alone; but if it dies, it produces much grain" (John 12:24).

If you are not willing to make the _____ in your marriage God requests, He cannot trust you with the greater _____ of the Kingdom.

Many times the adjustment to do the will of God means that you choose _____.

You as a couple cannot live in the _____ _____ and go with God at the same time.

Walking daily with the Lord requires _____ adjustments.

You have to remain _____ to the Lord to know _____ to make adjustments. The _____ is always what matters.

The same God who asked Peter to _____ is the

same God who asks you as a couple to _____.

A Man of sorrows and acquainted with grief (Isa. 53:3b).

Surely He has borne our griefs and carried our sorrows; yet we esteemed Him stricken, Smitten by God, and afflicted. But He was wounded for our transgressions, He was bruised for our iniquities; the chastisement for our peace was upon Him, and by His stripes we are healed. All we like sheep have gone astray; we have turned, every one, to his own way; and the Lord has laid on Him the iniquity of us all (Isa. 53:4-6).

To have the marriage/family Jesus wants for you may require

that you _____ _____ your life as He did.

Yet it pleased the Lord to bruise Him; He has put Him to grief. When You make His soul an offering for sin, He shall see His seed, He shall prolong His days, and the pleasure of the Lord shall prosper in His hand (Isa. 53:10).

65

Couple Talk 6

✛ **Use the following as a guide to talk with another couple or a small group of couples. Pray together as you begin your discussion.**

1. Reality 6 says: *You must make major adjustments in your life to join God in what He is doing.* What one thing from your life has demonstrated this reality that you would be willing to share with the group?

2. React to Henry Blackaby's statement: *If you are not willing to make the adjustments in your marriage God requests, He cannot trust you with the greater riches of the Kingdom.*

3. Luke 14:33 contains a word from Jesus to His followers. What implications does His statement have for married couples? " 'Whoever of you does not forsake all that he has cannot be My disciple' " (Luke 14:33).

4. Share with the group an experience in your marriage when you as a couple chose to make the adjustment that allowed you to follow God's will.

5. You have to remain close to the Lord to know when to make adjustments. How do you and your spouse maintain a close relationship with God?

6. Close by praying together the following passage from Isaiah.

Thank you God for your promise:
  " 'Fear not, for I am with you; be not dismayed, for I am your God.
  I will strengthen you, yes I help you, I will uphold you with My righteous
  right hand' " (Isa. 41:10).

Couple Shaper 6

Reality 6: *You must make major adjustments in your life to join God in what He is doing.*

Thoughts from Experiencing God
- When God speaks, revealing what He is about to do, that revelation is His invitation to adjust your life to God.
- The greatest single difficulty in following God may come at the point of adjustment.
- God is interested in absolute surrender to Him as Lord.
- You cannot stay where you are and go with God at the same time.
- The God who calls you is also the One who will enable you to adjust to His will.

What Kind of Adjustments?
Major adjustments in your life will come at the point of acting on your faith. When you face a crisis of belief, you must decide what you believe about God. That mental decision may be the easy part. The difficult part is adjusting your life to God and taking an action that demonstrates your faith. You may be called to attempt things only God can do.

Read the following Scriptures. What kind of adjustment was or is required in each? Match the Scripture with one or more of the categories. Write a letter or letters in each blank.

Scripture	Adjustments
_____ 1. Matthew 4:18-22	A. In circumstances
_____ 2. Matthew 5:43-48	B. In relationships
_____ 3. Matthew 6:5-8	C. In thinking
_____ 4. Matthew 20:20-28	D. In commitment
_____ 5. Acts 10:1-20	E. In actions
	F. In beliefs

Answers: 1-A; 2-B; 3-E; 4-B, C, or E; 5-C or F

67

Becoming Like Jesus

To have the marriage and family Jesus wants for you may require that you lay down your life as He did. That is the ultimate expression of becoming like Jesus. Isaiah 53:1-12 contains characteristics of Christ that provide a standard or plumb line for us. Read each verse below and sign the blank beside the verses that indicate a characteristic you have attained. Then review the ones you were not able to sign and pray for God's direction to attain them.

_____1 Who has believed our report? And to whom has the arm of the Lord been revealed?

_____2 For He shall grow up before Him as a tender plant, and as a root out of dry ground. He has no form or comeliness; and when we see Him, there is no beauty that we should desire Him.

_____3 He is despised and rejected by men, a Man of sorrows and acquainted with grief. And we hid, as it were, our faces from Him; He was despised, and we did not esteem Him.

_____4 Surely He has borne our griefs and carried our sorrows; yet we esteemed Him stricken, smitten by God, and afflicted.

_____5 But He was wounded for our transgressions, He was bruised for our iniquities; the chastisement for our peace was upon Him, and by His stripes we are healed.

_____6 All we like sheep have gone astray; we have turned, every one, to his own way; and the Lord had laid on Him the iniquity of us all.

_____7 He was oppressed and He was afflicted, yet He opened not His mouth; He was led as a lamb to the slaughter, and as a sheep before its shearers is silent, so He opened not His mouth.

_____8 He was taken from prison and from judgment, and who will declare His generation? For He was cut off from the land of the living; for the transgressions of My people He was stricken.

_____9 And they made His grave with the wicked-- but with rich at His death, because He had done no violence, nor was any deceit in His mouth.

_____10 Yet it pleased the Lord to bruise Him; He has put Him to grief. When You make His soul an offering for sin, He shall see His seed, He shall prolong His days, and the pleasure of the Lord shall prosper in His hand.

_____11 He shall see the labor of His soul, and be satisfied. By His knowledge My righteous Servant shall justify many, for He shall bear their iniquities.

_____12 Therefore I will divide Him a portion with the great, and He shall divide the spoil with the strong, because He poured out His soul unto death, and He was numbered with the transgressors, and He bore the sin of many, and made intercession for the transgressors.

Experiencing God as Couples Journal

What statement or Scripture in the video session has God used to speak to you about Himself, His purposes, or His ways?

_____

_____

_____

_____

_____

_____

Personalize the statement or Scripture by rewording it to reflect application to your marriage.

_____

_____

_____

_____

_____

_____

What adjustment is God leading you to make in response to what He has said to you?

_____

_____

_____

_____

_____

_____

How have you demonstrated your obedience to God this week?

_____

_____

_____

_____

_____

What particular person or concern has God given you a burden to pray with your spouse about?

_____

_____

_____

_____

_____

Couple Time 6

1. Consider the following areas of your life as a couple and discuss what adjustments may be required for you to follow God's will. Make notes in the space provided.

- Circumstances (job, home, finances, and others)
- Relationships (family, friends, business associates, and others)
- Thinking (prejudices, methods, your potential, and others)
- Commitments (to family, church, job, plans, tradition, and others)
- Actions (how you pray, give, serve, and others)
- Beliefs (about God, His purposes, His ways, your relationship with Him, and others)

_____

_____

_____

_____

_____

2. Review the exercise in Couple Shaper 6 where you evaluated your life using Isaiah 53:1-12. Share with each other your responses.

3. Are you as a couple willing to face what you know to be the will of God and make the adjustments (even if it didn't or doesn't work the first time) necessary to follow Him?

❏ Yes, we are   ❏ No, not sure

4. Share with each other what you recorded in your *Experiencing God as Couples Journal.* Close your time together in prayer for each other and your marriage.

Allowing God to Work Through Your Marriage

REALITY 7

You come to know God by experience as you obey Him and He accomplishes His work through you.

Jesus answered and said to him, "If anyone loves Me, he will keep My word; and My Father will love him, and We will come to him and make Our home with him."

–John 14:23

Couple View 7

"Call upon Me in the day of trouble; I will deliver you, and you shall glorify me" (Ps. 50:15).

In times of trouble, call _____ on Him and let

Him _____ you and _____ Him.

" 'But why do you call Me "Lord, Lord," and not do the things which I say? Whoever comes to Me and hears My sayings and does them, I will show you whom he is like' " (Luke 6:46-47).

Your house (home) will withstand the storms when you

_____ _____ to Him, _____

what He says, and _____ what He says.

" 'Whoever comes to Me, and hears My sayings and does them, I will show you whom he is like: He is like a man building a house, who dug deep and laid the foundation on the rock. And when the flood arose, the stream beat vehemently against that house, and could not shake it, for it was founded on the rock. But he who heard and did nothing is like a man who built a house on the earth without a foundation, against which the stream beat vehemently; and immediately it fell. And the ruin of that house was great' " (Luke 6:47-49).

When you obey God in the middle of a crisis, it puts you in

the _____ of God's activity.

"So Samuel said: 'Has the Lord as great delight in burnt offerings and sacrifices, as in obeying the voice of the Lord? Behold, to obey is better than sacrifice, and to heed than the fat of rams. For rebellion is as the sin of witchcraft, and stubbornness is as iniquity and idolatry. Because you have rejected the word of the Lord, He also has rejected you from being king' " (1 Sam. 15:22-23).

Of all the things you offer God, there is no substitute for simple, clear _____.

There is a direct _____ between your obedience and what happens in your _____.

Obedience is the absolute _____ for putting you in the middle of God's activity.

You can tell if you are being _____ by looking to see what God is doing out of your obedience.

The _____ of opportunity for obedience concerning your family is _____.

When you take the _____ of obedience, God will show

you what He had in mind while you were going through the

_____.

Sometimes spouses must help each other understand the

_____ aspects of obedience.

When God reveals what He wants one spouse to do, He also

_____ the other.

You'll never _____ what God has in mind for you as a

couple unless you _____ _____ to the next step of obedience.

Our responsibility is to put _____ first, above all else.

"God is our refuge and strength, a very present help in trouble. Therefore we will not fear" (Ps. 46:1-2a).

If God asks you to do something, He will _____ through
it with you.

Whatever God is asking you as a couple to do, _____ _____

and do it.

"There is no fear in love; but perfect love casts out fear, because fear involves torment. But he who fears has not been made perfect in love" (1 John 4:18).

If you have fear during your obedience to God, _____

your love relationship with your Lord.

" "He who has My commandments and keeps them, it is he who loves Me. And he who loves Me will be loved by My Father, and I will love him and manifest Myself to him.' ... Jesus answered and said to him, 'If anyone loves Me, he will keep My word; and My Father will love him, and We will come to him and make Our home with him. He who does not love Me does not keep My words; and the word which you hear is not Mine but the Father's who sent Me" (John 14:21, 23-24).

Reality 1: *God is always at work around you.*
Reality 2: *God pursues a love relationship with you that is real and personal.*
Reality 3: *God invites you to become involved with Him in His work.*
Reality 4: *God speaks by the Holy Spirit through the Bible, prayer, circumstances, and the church to reveal Himself, His purposes, and His ways.*
Reality 5: *God's invitation for you to work with Him always leads you to a crisis of belief that requires faith and action.*
Reality 6: *You must make major adjustments in your life to join God in what He is doing.*
Reality 7: *You come to know God by experience as you obey Him and He accomplishes His work through you.*

Couple Talk 7

✣ **Use the following as a guide to talk with another couple or a small group of couples. Pray together as you begin your discussion.**

1. Reality 7 says: *You come to know God by experience as you obey Him and He accomplishes His work through you.* What one thing from your life has demonstrated this reality that you would be willing to share with the group?

2. Give testimony to the significance of the following statements made during the video session:

- When you obey God in the middle of a crisis, it puts you in the mainstream of God's activity.
- Of all the things you offer God, there is no substitute for simple, clear obedience.
- There is a direct connection between your obedience and what happens in your family.

3. Share a time when you and your spouse helped each other understand the practical aspects of obeying God. What happened when you as a couple obeyed God?

4. Review all seven realities. Share with the group which of the seven has been a spiritual breakthrough for you over the past several weeks. How has it affected your marriage?

5. Close your group time by encouraging each person to pray for a specific concern in another person's life.

Couple Shaper 7

Reality 7: *You come to know God by experience as you obey Him and He accomplishes His work through you.*

Thoughts from Experiencing God
• Obedience means doing what God commands.
• Obedience is costly.
• Obedience requires total dependence on God to work through you.
• Waiting on God is always worth the wait.
• If you love God, you will obey Him. Obedience is an outward expression of your love of God.
• God blesses those who are obedient to Him.

Obedience Is Your Moment of Truth
Obedience is your moment of truth. What you do will:
• reveal what you believe about Jesus.
• determine whether you will experience Jesus' mighty work in and through you.
• determine whether you will come to know Jesus more intimately.

Read 1 John 2:3-6 below. Circle the word *know* each time it occurs. Underline the words *obey* and *obeys*. Draw a box enclosing the word *love*.

"By this we know that we know Him, of we keep His commandments. He who says, 'I know him,' and does not keep His commandments, is a liar, and the truth is not in him. But whoever keeps His word, truly the love of God is perfected in him. By this we know that we are in Him. He who says he abides in Him ought himself to walk just as He walked" (1 John 2:3-6).

When you come to a moment of truth when you must choose whether to obey God, you cannot obey Him unless you believe and trust Him. You cannot believe and trust Him unless you love Him. You cannot love Him unless you know Him.

Obedience Is...
What is obedience? Check one.
☐ Saying you will do what is commanded.
☐ Doing what is commanded.

God's commands are not given so you can pick and choose the ones you want to obey and forget about the rest. God wants you to obey all His commands out of your love relationship with Him. When He sees you are faithful in a little, God will be able to trust you with more. And the results will be joy in your life and uninterrupted fellowship with God.

Obey God and Accomplish Much
When you obey God, He will accomplish through you what He has purposed to do. When God does something through your life and marriage that only He can do, you will come to know Him more intimately. If you do not obey Him, you will miss out on some of the most exciting experiences of your life.

Read Exodus 7:1-6.

What was Moses commanded to do? _____

_____

What did God say He was going to do? _____

_____

What would be the result when Moses obeyed and God did

what He said? _____

_____

This pattern can be seen throughout Moses' life.
• God invited Moses to join Him in what He was doing to deliver Israel.
• God told Moses what he was to do.
• Moses obeyed.
• God accomplished what He purposed to do.
• Moses and those around him came to know God more dearly and intimately.

Can you substitute you name for Moses' name? If you are obedient, God will work some wonderful things through you. You will come to know Him in a way that will bring rejoicing to your life.

Experiencing God as Couples Journal
What statement or Scripture in the video session has God used to speak to you about Himself, His purposes, or His ways?

_____

_____

_____

_____

_____

_____

Personalize the statement or Scripture by rewording it to reflect application to your marriage.

_____

_____

_____

_____

_____

_____

_____

What adjustment is God leading you to make in response to what He has said to you?

_____

_____

_____

_____

_____

_____

How have you demonstrated your obedience to God this week?

_____

_____

_____

_____

What particular person or concern has God given you a burden to pray with your spouse about?

_____

_____

_____

_____

_____

Couple Time 7

1. Henry Blackaby said in the video session that, "The window of opportunity for obedience concerning your family is narrow." Discuss the implications of this for your family.

2. Your responsibility is to put God first, above all else. You'll never know what God has in mind for you as a couple unless you go on to the step of obedience. Share an area of your life as a couple where you know this is true. What adjustments need to be made for you to obey God?

3. Talk with each other about the sense of joy and freedom that comes when you obey God. Think back on experiences in your marriage when that was true.

4. Review the seven realities of experiencing God. Read them together as a couple substituting *we* for *you*.

5. Share with each other what you recorded in your *Experiencing God as Couples Journal*. Close your time together in prayer for each other and your marriage.

Committing to a Covenant Marriage

And the Lord God caused a deep sleep to fall over Adam, and he
slept; and He took one of his ribs, and closed up the flesh in its
place. Then the rib which the Lord God had taken from man He
made into a woman, and He brought her to the man. And Adam
said: "This is now bone of my bones and flesh of my flesh; she
shall be called Woman, because she was taken out of Man."
Therefore a man shall leave his father and mother and be joined
to his wife, and they shall become one flesh.

—Genesis 2:21-24

Couple View 8

The first symbol of God's covenant with His people was the

_____.

"When Abram was ninety-nine years old, the Lord appeared to Abram and said to him, 'I am Almighty God; walk before Me and be blameless. And I will make My covenant between Me and you, and will multiply you exceedingly.' Then Abram fell on his face, and God talked with him, saying: 'As for Me, behold, My covenant is with you, and you shall be a father of many nations' " (Gen. 17:1-4).

"I will establish My covenant between Me and you and your descendants after you in their generations, for an everlasting covenant, to be God to you and your descendants after you" (Gen. 17:7).

The covenant you as a couple make _____ your children,

your grandchildren, and the families around you.

"As they were eating, Jesus took bread, blessed and broke it, and gave it to the disciples and said, 'Take, eat; this is My body.' Then He took the cup, and gave thanks, and gave it to them, saying, 'Drink from it, all of you. For this is My blood of the new covenant, which is shed for many for the remission of sins' " (Matt. 26:26-28).

The cross became the symbol of the covenant relationship of

_____ God established through Christ.

God provides all the _____ of Heaven for the

Christian family.

" 'All things that the Father has are Mine. Therefore I said that He will take of Mine and declare it to you' " (John 16:15).

As His divine power has given to us all things that pertain to life and godliness, through the knowledge of Him who called us by glory and virtue (2 Peter 1:3).

The symbol of a _____ marriage is the wedding ring.

I gladly and joyfully / renew my marriage vow to you. / As your marriage partner, / I pledge to you my faithfulness / to love, honor / and to keep you in sickness and in health / for richer or for poorer / to live according to God's Word / under the Lordship of Christ / and the enabling of the Holy Spirit / and to keep faithfully unto you / as long as we both shall live.

Believing that marriage is a covenant intended by God to be a lifelong relationship between a man and a woman, we vow to God, each other, our families, and our community to remain steadfast in unconditional love, reconciliation, and sexual purity, while purposefully growing in our covenant marriage relationship.

85

Couple Talk 8

✛ **During this Couple Talk, you and another couple or a small group of couples will experience what you viewed during the video session as couples participated in a time of commitment. Pray together as you begin.**

1. Read the following Scripture.

So God created man in His own image, in the image of God He created him; male and female He created them. Then God blessed them, and God said to them, "Be fruitful and multiply; fill the earth and subdue it" (Genesis 1:27-28a).

And the Lord God caused a deep sleep to fall over Adam, and he slept; and He took one of his ribs, and closed up the flesh in its place. Then the rib which the Lord God had taken from man He made into a woman, and He brought her to the man. And Adam said: "This is now bone of my bones and flesh of my flesh; she shall be called Woman, because she was taken out of Man." Therefore a man shall leave his father and mother and be joined to his wife, and they shall become one flesh (Genesis 2:21-24).

2. Invite each couple to light a candle, hold right hands, and repeat the following as a recommitment of their wedding vows.

I gladly and joyfully / renew my marriage vow to you. / As your marriage partner, / I pledge to you my faithfulness / to love, honor / and to keep you in sickness and in health / for richer or for poorer / to live according to God's Word / under the Lordship of Christ / and the enabling of the Holy Spirit / and to keep faithfully unto you / as long as we both shall live.

3. Invite each couple to turn to page 94 in this book and read together the commitment to a Covenant Marriage. Encourage them to pray about the pledge and then sign and date it if they want it to be the foundation of their marriage. Further instructions on what they can do with the signed commitment will be made in Couple Time 8.

4. Close the recommitment time by inviting couples to share what this study has meant over the past few weeks and what it will mean to them in the future. Pray together asking God to bless and guide each marriage represented in the group.

Couple Shaper 8

Now that you have considered the seven realities of experiencing God, it is appropriate to conclude your study with a commitment to a godly marriage. This Couple Shaper will be a little different than the others as you consider what it means to have a covenant marriage. Work through the following material and then discuss it with your spouse during Couple Time 8.

Committing to a Covenant Marriage

Most of us probably don't fully grasp the magnitude of what we are saying when we repeat our wedding vows. In our mind's eye we are committing ourselves to a lifelong relationship with our spouses. However, marriage today is seen as a legal contract based on rights and responsibilities rather than a covenant based on unconditional love. A legal contract is necessary to begin and likewise to end a marriage. But a covenant is more than a contract.

What is the difference between a covenant and a contract? List characteristics of each in the space provided.

Contract: _____

Covenant: _____

A contract is a legal agreement stipulating that if one party will live up to certain terms, the other party will deliver comparable services. If either party fails to meet the requirements, the contract is null and void. A covenant is more than a declaration of interdependence. A covenant is intended by God to be a lifelong relationship exemplifying unconditional love, reconciliation, sexual purity, and growth. A covenant is an eternal commitment with God. People can negotiate out of contracts, but not out of a covenant. The heart of covenant marriage is "the steadfast love of the Lord," which comes from the very heart of God and "never ceases" (Lamentations 3:22).

Though our intentions are good when we marry, we have no perception of the depth of the unconditional love necessary to uphold these commitments to which we are agreeing. Our promises have not been tried and tested by time and turmoil.

The value of a "covenant marriage relationship" as opposed to a "contractual marriage agreement" lies in a person's understanding and acceptance of God's intent for marriage and of the value of a "covenant." Whereas a contract is based on rights and responsibilities and is motivated by self-centeredness; a covenant is based on unconditional love which comes from God and can only be empowered by God's presence in the marriage.

God's Intent for Marriage

God intends for marriage to be a lifelong covenant relationship between a man and a woman. When a couple shares their wedding vows, they are pledging to God, each other, their families, and their community to remain steadfast in unconditional love, reconciliation, and sexual purity, while purposefully growing in their covenant marriage relationship. It is God's desire to bring wholeness to families through covenant marriage relationships.

Genesis 1:27 says that, "God created man in His own image; in the image of God He created him; male and female He created them. Then God blessed them, and God said to them, 'Be fruitful and multiply, fill the earth, and subdue it; and have dominion over … every living thing that moves on the earth.' " When God "blessed them" He initiated an action and then empowered the man and woman to complete the action. God gave them the gift of a covenant relationship and then equipped them to be successful.

In Genesis 2:18,22-25 God acknowledged that, " 'It is not good that man should be alone; I will make him a helper comparable to him.' … Then the rib which the Lord God had taken from man He made into a woman, and He brought her to the man. And Adam said: 'This is now bone of my bones and flesh of my flesh; she shall be called Woman, because she was taken out of Man.' Therefore a man shall leave his father and mother and be joined to his wife, and they shall become one flesh. And they were both naked, the man and his wife, and were not ashamed." In the context of a covenant relationship, God provided the ultimate experience in "oneness" through sexual intimacy.

Proverbs 18:22 says, "He who finds a wife finds a good thing, and obtains favor from the Lord." How do you perceive your marriage? Men, do you believe God brought your wife to you? Do you consider her a gift from God? Have you considered that when God brought her to you He was expressing His love to you? God was saying, "It is not good that you should be alone so I have made a helper for you as an expression of my love for you and you are to love her as I have loved my bride, the church. You shall readily lay down your life for her, loving her as you love yourself."

This same attitude is appropriate for husbands and wives. Write a letter in the space below or on a separate sheet of paper to your spouse expressing your thanks for God's gift to you.

_____

_____

_____

_____

_____

_____

When the term "covenant" is used in the Bible it is evident that God is the one who initiates the covenant. God established His covenant with the patriarchs of our faith. God said to Noah, "Behold I myself do establish My covenant with you, and with your descendants after you" (Genesis 9:9, NASB). God said to Abraham, "I will establish My covenant between Me and you, and I will multiply you exceedingly ... God said, 'As for Me, behold, My covenant is with you and you shall be the father of a multitude of nations' " (Genesis 17:2,4, NASB).

God is always the giver of the covenant. We are the recipients of the covenant. We choose to accept it and remain obedient to the covenant God has established. The foundation for such a covenant is unconditional love, for that is who God is. Our covenant relationship with our spouse should reflect, and in actuality can only be made possible through, God's gift of unconditional love.

Covenant Marriages Are a Model for the World

If you believe that God brought the two of you together and that your marriage was not a coincidence, then how you live your life reflects that belief. God has a plan for your marriage. He desires to see your love grow and bear fruit. The goal of a covenant marriage is not to merely enjoy each other's company nor is it to simply endure to the end. The goal of a covenant marriage is to glorify God in your relationship and to exemplify Christ to the world.

You and your spouse can begin by exemplifying a positive attitude about marriage. In a day when researchers are tracking negative social trends such as the increase in divorce rates, cohabitation, out-of-wedlock births, and single-parent households, focus on the positive attributes of marriage. As you do, consider the following suggestions.

❏ As individuals, evaluate your present lifestyle and relationships based on God's Word.

❏ If you are divorced and there is the possibility for reconciliation, seek God's will in reconciling with your spouse. If that is not possible, ask for God's forgiveness and direction in accordance with His Word and the church.

❏ If you know a couple preparing for marriage, encourage them to prayerfully consider the use of the covenant marriage pledge as a guide in their marriage preparation. The pledge may also be incorporated into their wedding ceremony.

❏ Affirm the covenant pledge you made during your small group time and pray that God will enable you to remain true to the covenant.

❏ Take the necessary steps to strengthen your covenant relationship with your spouse. Seek assistance from your congregational leadership to discover the various opportunities available to you to accomplish this goal.

❏ Encourage and support your congregational leaders as they set the pace in leading your congregation to become a covenant marriage congregation.

Experiencing God as Couples Journal
What statement or Scripture in the video session has God used to speak to you about Himself, His purposes, or His ways?

_____

_____

_____

_____

_____

_____

Personalize the statement or Scripture by rewording it to reflect application to your marriage.

_____

_____

_____

_____

_____

_____

What adjustment is God leading you to make in response to what He has said to you?

_____

_____

_____

_____

_____

_____

How have you demonstrated your obedience to God this week?

_____

_____

_____

_____

What particular person or concern has God given you a burden to pray with your spouse about?

_____

_____

_____

_____

Couple Time 8

1. Focus on experiencing God as a couple. Give an example of how the seven realities of experiencing God has been evident to you as an individual and how each has affected you as a couple.

2. Discuss as a couple what it means to each of you to sign the covenant marriage commitment. How will it impact your marriage in the days, months, and years ahead? Join other couples in celebrating the activity of God in marriages and communities by registering your commitment with the Covenant Marriage Movement office. (One of the goals is to document the number of couples in our nation and around the world who have taken a stand on behalf of Covenant Marriage.) Two copies of the commitment card are located on page 94. Keep one copy for yourself. Mail the other copy or a photocopy to Covenant Marriage Movement; 127 Ninth Avenue, North; Nashville, TN 37234-0151; or fax it to 615-251-5058; or email your decision to *covenantmarriage@lifeway.com*. For more information about the movement, call 1-800-268-1343.

3. What specific actions will you take as a couple as a result of signing the covenant marriage commitment card. Review the list on pages 90-91 and prayerfully consider each one. Check those that you will act on in your marriage. And then, do it!

4. Close your time together with a prayer of thanksgiving for your marriage and a commitment to God and each other to draw closer to God individually and as a couple

OUR COVENANT MARRIAGE

Believing that marriage is a covenant intended by God to be a lifelong relationship between a man and a woman, we vow to God, each other, our families, and our community to remain steadfast in unconditional love, reconciliation, and sexual purity, while purposefully growing in our covenant-marriage relationship.

_____   _____
Name   Date

_____   _____
Name   Date

OUR COVENANT MARRIAGE

Believing that marriage is a covenant intended by God to be a lifelong relationship between a man and a woman, we vow to God, each other, our families, and our community to remain steadfast in unconditional love, reconciliation, and sexual purity, while purposefully growing in our covenant-marriage relationship.

_____   _____
Name   Date

_____   _____
Name   Date

CHRISTIAN GROWTH STUDY PLAN

Preparing Christians to Serve

In the **Christian Growth Study Plan (formerly Church Study Course)**, this book *Experiencing God as Couples* is a resource for course credit in the subject area Home/Family of the Christian Growth category of diploma plans. To receive credit, read the book, complete the learning activities, show your work to your pastor, a staff member or church leader, then complete the following information. This page may be duplicated. Send the completed page to:

Christian Growth Study Plan
127 Ninth Avenue, North, MSN 117
Nashville, TN 37234-0117
FAX: (615)251-5067
For information about the Christian Growth Study Plan, refer to the current Christian Growth Study Plan Catalog. Your church office may have a copy. If not, request a free copy from the Christian Growth Study Plan office (615/251-2525).

Experiencing God as Couples
CG-0517

PARTICIPANT INFORMATION

Social Security Number (USA ONLY)	Personal CGSP Number*	Date of Birth (MONTH, DAY, YEAR)

Name (First, Middle, Last)		Home Phone

Address (Street, Route, or P.O. Box)	City, State, or Province	Zip/Postal Code

CHURCH INFORMATION

Church Name

Address (Street, Route, or P.O. Box)	City, State, or Province	Zip/Postal Code

CHANGE REQUEST ONLY

☐ Former Name

☐ Former Address	City, State, or Province	Zip/Postal Code

☐ Former Church	City, State, or Province	Zip/Postal Code

Signature of Pastor, Conference Leader, or Other Church Leader	Date

*New participants are requested but not required to give SS# and date of birth. Existing participants, please give CGSP# when using SS# for the first time. Thereafter, only one ID# is required. **Mail to:** Christian Growth Study Plan, 127 Ninth Ave., North, Nashville, TN 37234-0117. Fax: (615)251-5067

Rev. 6-99